Rainbows and Hot Air Balloons

A true story

Story by
Jennifer Cooke

•

Illustrations by
Craig Cameron

BELLE ISLE BOOKS
www.belleislebooks.com

Copyright 2016 by Jennifer Cooke. No portion of this book may be reproduced or transmitted in any form whatsoever without prior written permission from the publisher, except in the case of brief quotations published in articles and reviews.

ISBN: 978-1-9399307-2-9

Library of Congress Control Number: 2016942642

Printed in the United States

Published by

BELLE ISLE BOOKS
www.belleislebooks.com

For Nanny and Pop-Pop.
-J.C.
For Grandma and Papa.
-C.C.

I always have a hard time using my hands to hold my spoon ... Nanny says it's because I have "morning hands."

When it's time to go to school, I get my lunchbox, and Nanny makes me stop at the door so she can take my picture.

When we go outside, we always see a rainbow or a hot air balloon. It's like magic!

Then we get in Nanny's little silver car and we head off to school. She calls it the "silver bullet."

When I get home, I go out to Pop-Pop's work shed and he gives me a piece of wood and some nails and a hammer.

Pop-Pop hangs the awards that I get from school on the walls in his shed.

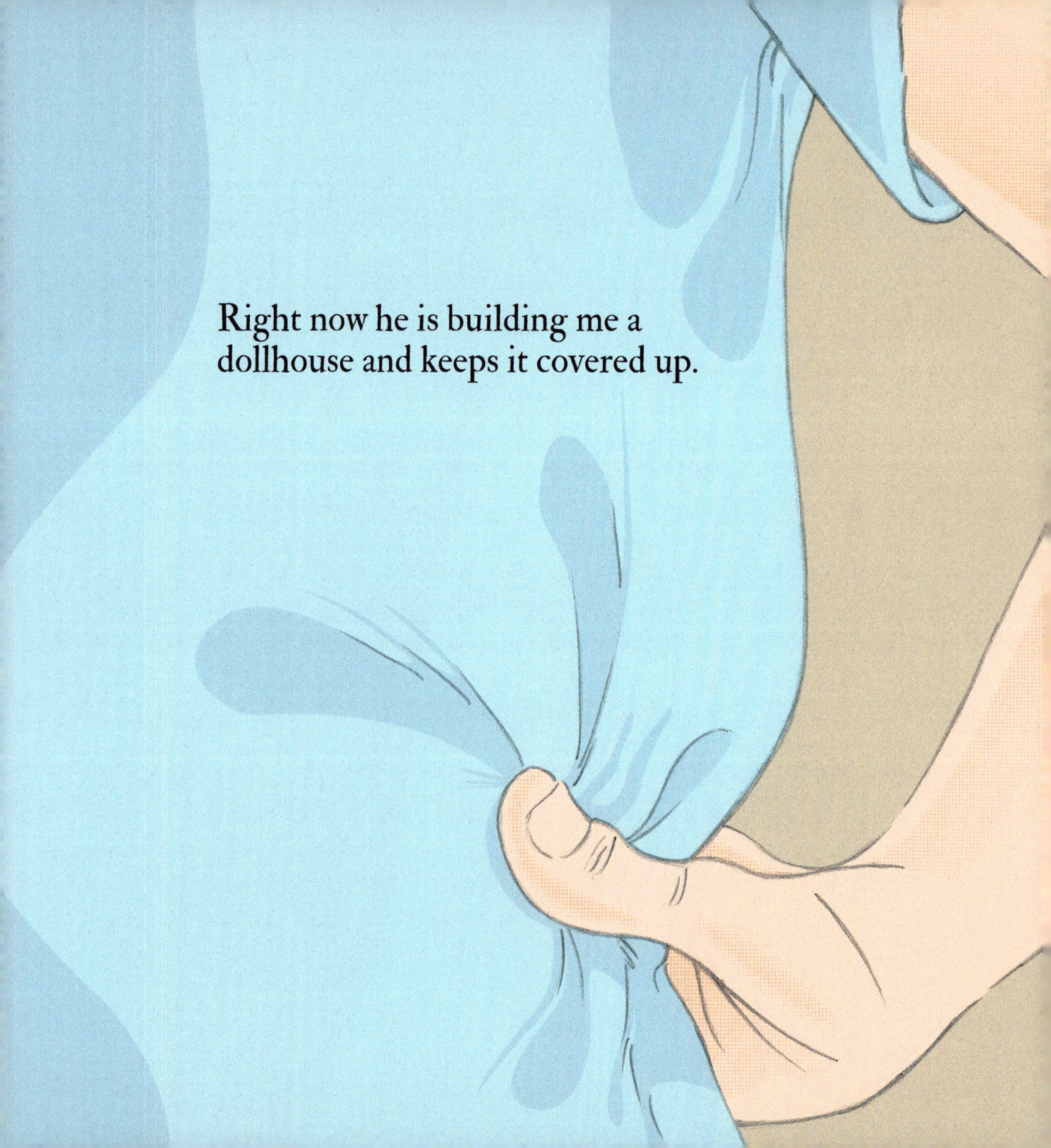

Right now he is building me a dollhouse and keeps it covered up.

I'm not supposed to peek.

Pop-Pop and I stay outside until Nanny yells at us through the window to come inside. She calls, "Yooo Hooo, come inside for dinner, you two."

At night after I've eaten dinner, I take a bath and Nanny reminds me to wash behind my ears.

Then I get into bed and Nanny tucks me in. After I'm all tucked in, she turns off the light and tries to find me in the dark to give me a kiss. I always get the giggles because she can never find me.

Acknowledgements

I would like to thank my father, John Cooke, whose enthusiasm for this project was unmatched by anyone else, even myself. Thank you for everything. I would also like to thank Helen Parmelee, Nathan Culver, Linda Culver, and Theresa and Rich Guernsey for their love and support. I would like to thank all of my family and friends who contributed to our campaign. You amazed us with your generous support.

— Jennifer Cooke

I would like to thank my family and friends for your support through this wonderful experience. I would also like to thank everyone who supported this book by contributing to our campaign.

We would both like to thank Robert Pruett and everyone at Brandylane Publishers for guiding us through our first publishing experience. Special thanks to our friend, Beth Malone, for bringing us together and inspiring us to collaborate on *Rainbows and Hot Air Balloons*. We wouldn't have a book without you.

— Craig Cameron

About the Author

JENNIFER COOKE earned a Master of Social Work degree from Georgia State University and has since worked with children in different capacities, including as a mental health counselor and as a nanny. *Rainbows and Hot Air Balloons* is her first children's book.

About the Illustrator

CRAIG CAMERON is an Atlanta-based illustrator and arts administrator. He received his BFA from Georgia Southern University. He exhibits work at various galleries throughout Atlanta and has also worked with art organizations such as Dashboard and the Atlanta Printmakers Studio. *Rainbows and Hot Air Balloons* is his first children's book.

CPSIA information can be obtained
at www.ICGtesting.com
Printed in the USA
LVOW06*1353120916
504256LV00003B/6/P